AF270362

Emergency Trucks

Julie Murray

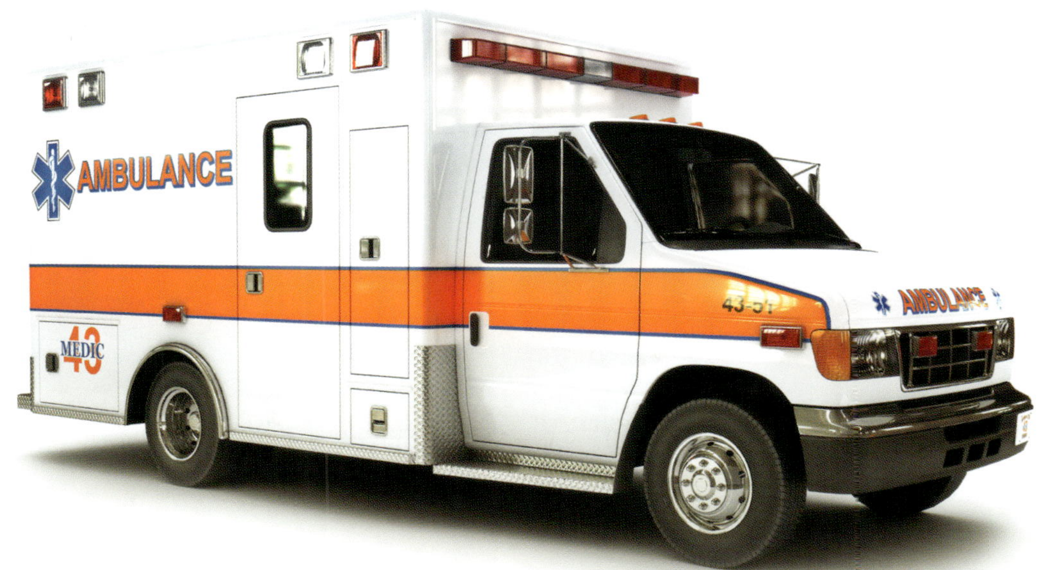

Abdo Kids Junior
is an Imprint of Abdo Kids
abdobooks.com

Abdo
TRUCKS AT WORK
Kids

abdobooks.com

Published by Abdo Kids, a division of ABDO, P.O. Box 398166, Minneapolis, Minnesota 55439.
Copyright © 2024 by Abdo Consulting Group, Inc. International copyrights reserved in all countries.
No part of this book may be reproduced in any form without written permission from the publisher.
Abdo Kids Junior™ is a trademark and logo of Abdo Kids.

Printed in the United States of America, North Mankato, Minnesota.

052023

092023

THIS BOOK CONTAINS
RECYCLED MATERIALS

Photo Credits: Getty Images, Shutterstock, ©Washington State DOT p.22/ CC BY-NC-ND 2.0,
©Dawn Endico p.22/ CC BY-SA 2.0

Production Contributors: Teddy Borth, Jennie Forsberg, Grace Hansen

Design Contributors: Candice Keimig, Pakou Moua

Library of Congress Control Number: 2022946713
Publisher's Cataloging-in-Publication Data

Names: Murray, Julie, author.

Title: Emergency trucks / by Julie Murray

Description: Minneapolis, Minnesota : Abdo Kids, 2024 | Series: Trucks at work | Includes online resources
    and index.

Identifiers: ISBN 9781098266134 (lib. bdg.) | ISBN 9781098266837 (ebook) | ISBN 9781098267186
    (Read-to-me ebook)

Subjects: LCSH: Trucks--Juvenile literature. | Vehicles--Juvenile literature. | Emergency vehicles--Juvenile
    literature.

Classification: DDC 388.32--dc23

Table of Contents

Emergency Trucks

Mary sees flashing lights.

It is an emergency truck!

POLICE
POLICE
Aventura
POLICE

A house is on fire. A fire
truck is there to help.

LSFD
15
15

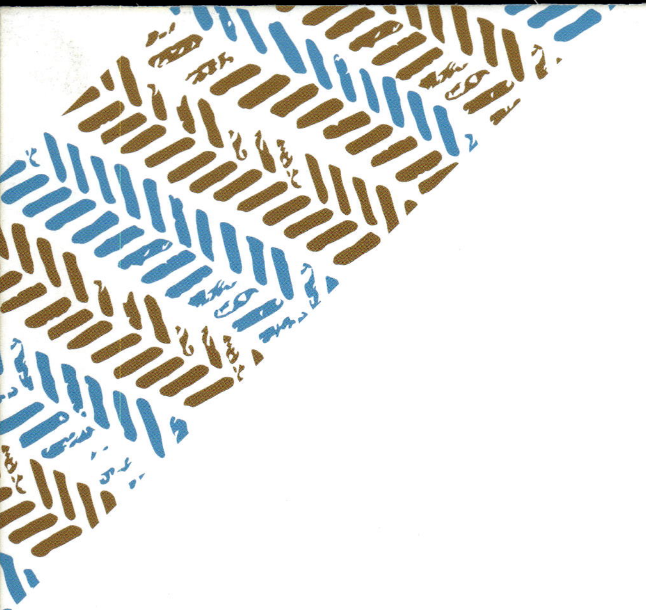

The ambulance truck moves hurt people to a hospital.

PARAMEDIC

Ed's car broke down.

He called a tow truck.

RUBICON
Jeep
SERVING BROOKINGS, GOLD BEACH, AND PORT ORFORD
AAA
Emergency
Services
24-HOUR SERVICE
11

Eva drives a police truck.

She keeps people safe.

2205
EMERGENCY
911
2205
HOLLYWOOD
POLICE
Professionally Accredited
CITY

A water tender brings water

to a fire.

GINE 49
911
PLAINSBORO FD
-ONE

There was a bad accident.

A **heavy rescue** truck helps.

HIAB
X-HIPRO 418

A **SWAT** truck is armored. It helps in unsafe situations.

S.W.A.T

What emergency trucks
have you seen?

AMBULANCE

More Emergency Trucks

air supply truck

hazardous material truck

ladder truck

roadside assistance truck

Glossary

heavy rescue

a response vehicle with tools and equipment to support rescue operations.

SWAT

short for Special Weapons and Tactics.

Index

Visit **abdokids.com** to access crafts, games, videos, and more!